THE **C** **E** BOOK

SIMON & SCHUSTER BOOKS FOR YOUNG READERS

Simon & Schuster Building, Rockefeller Center, 1230 Avenue of the Americas, New York, New York 10020
Illustrations and design copyright © 1990 by Hannah Tofts. Text and compilation copyright © 1990 by Two-Can Publishing Ltd. All rights reserved including the right of reproduction in whole or in part in any form. Originally published in Great Britain by Two-Can Publishing Ltd. First U.S. edition 1991. SIMON & SCHUSTER BOOKS FOR YOUNG READERS is a trademark of Simon & Schuster. Manufactured in Hong Kong.

10 9 8 7 6 5 4 3 2 1   (pbk.) 10 9 8 7 6 5 4 3 2 1

Library of Congress Cataloging-in-Publication Data: Tofts, Hannah. The collage book / by Hannah Tofts ; written and edited by Diane James ; photography by Jon Barnes. Includes index. Summary: Surveys a variety of collage projects and techniques. 1. Collage— Technique—Juvenile literature. [1. Collage.] I. James. Diane. II. Barnes, Jon, ill. III. Title. N7433.7.T6 1991 90-47122 702'.8'12—dc20 CIP AC

ISBN 0-671-73888-7   ISBN 0-671-73889-5 (pbk.)

P9-DTR-214

EQUIPMENT

In this book you will find lots of ideas for making different types of collage. A collage is a picture built up from pieces of paper, fabric, wood, or odds and ends that you glue onto a backing sheet. You should be able to find most of the equipment you need around the house. When using glue to attach heavy objects, read the directions carefully. Always ask a grown-up for help when cutting and gluing.

Start a collection of odds and ends such as fabric scraps, buttons, pieces of ribbon and cord, pictures cut from magazines, stamps, photographs, and cardboard tubes.

awl (for making holes)

glue (read the instructions carefully and ask a grown-up for help)

scissors

Scotch ™ tape

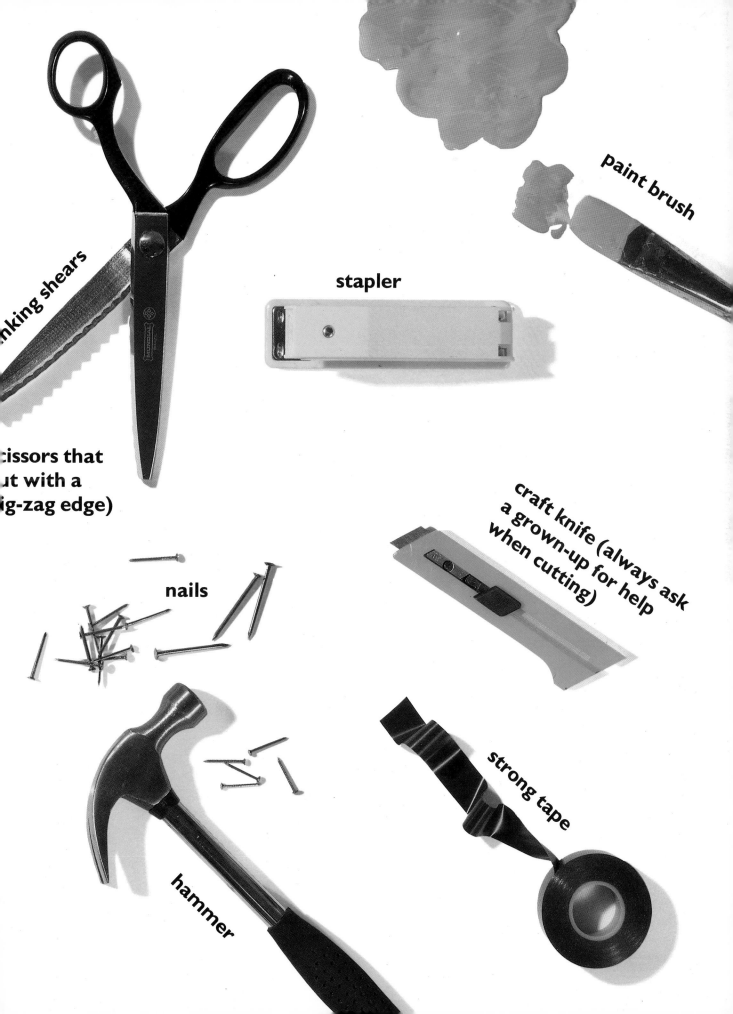

paint brush

inking shears

stapler

**cissors that
ut with a
ig-zag edge)**

**craft knife (always ask
a grown-up for help
when cutting)**

nails

strong tape

hammer

Try making a sampler from the odds and ends you have collected. Look for paper with interesting textures and patterns. Use thick cardboard or paper for the base. Arrange your collection on the base and move things around until you are happy with the way it looks. Glue a small area at a time.

Here are some ideas for making a collage with raised surfaces. Look for small cardboard boxes, tubes, egg cartons and corrugated cardboard.

You can give paper a raised surface by scoring, pleating and curling. Wrap a long strip of paper tightly around a pencil. Pull it off gently and you will have a perfect curl. Use a ruler and scoring tool to score lines on strips of paper. Fold the paper into pleats along the score lines.

Arrange the pieces on strong cardboard and glue them in position.

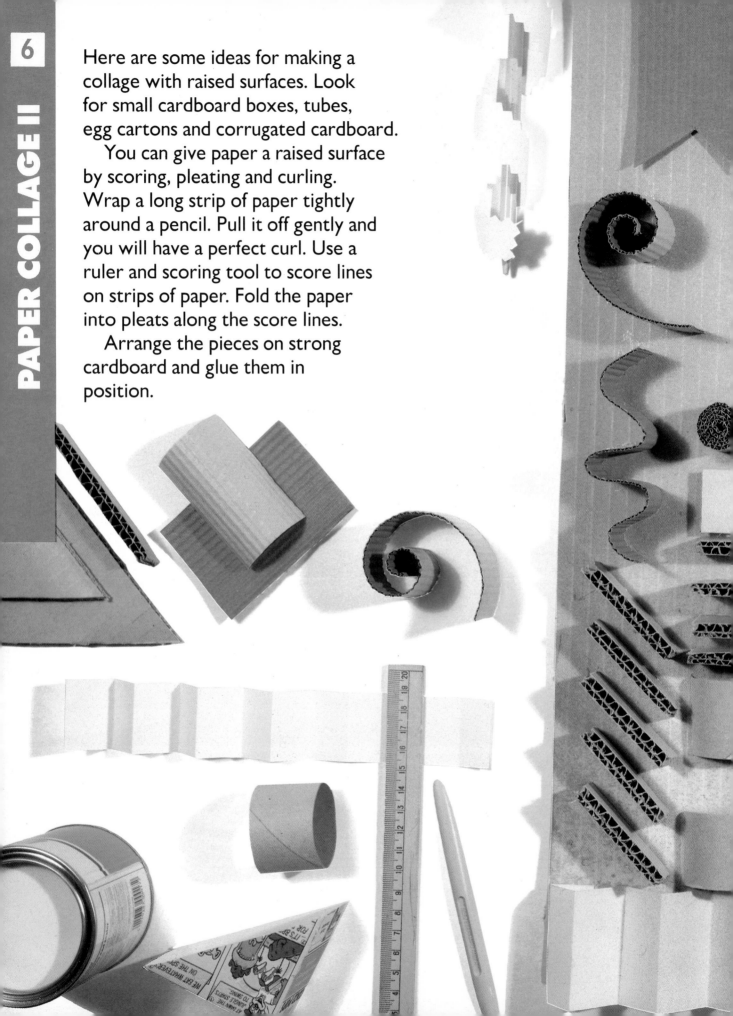

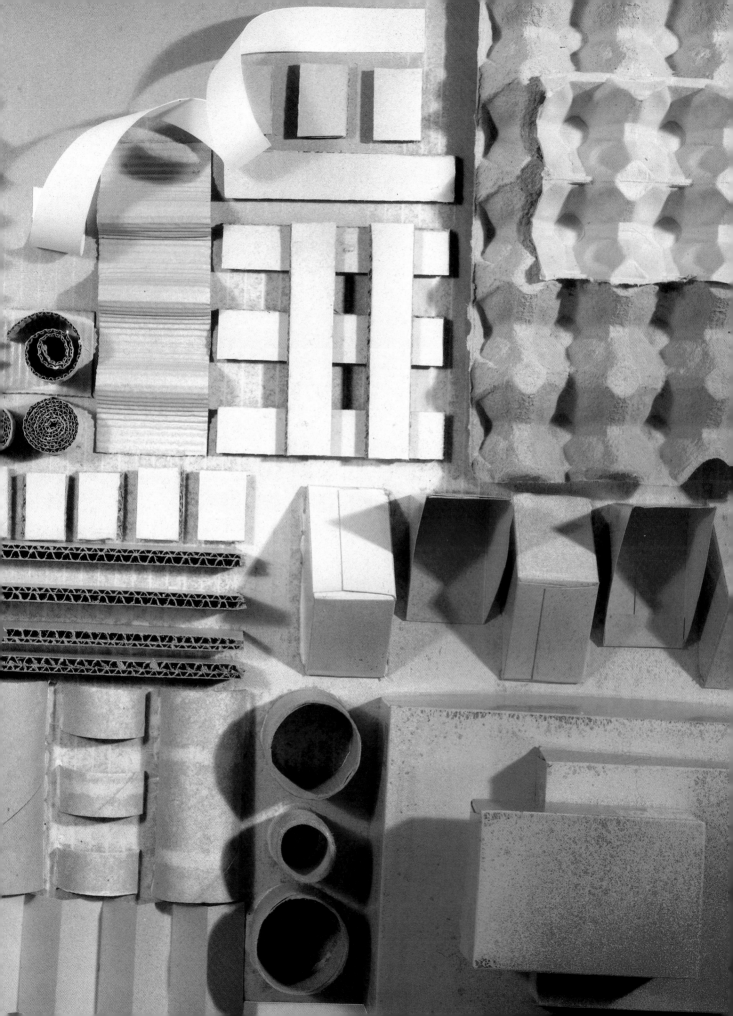

For this collage we have used color photographs and pictures cut from magazines. Our theme was animals but you can choose your own.

You can carefully cut around the pictures or tear them out to get a rough edge. Look for pictures with unusual textures.

To make paper stand out from the background, glue pictures onto thick cardboard before attaching.

Give old jugs, jars, vases and frames a new look by gluing on scraps of paper to decorate them. Work out a color scheme before you start and arrange your collection of torn or cut paper scraps. You could also use stamps or pictures cut from old magazines.

Use watered-down white glue to attach the pieces of paper to the object.

By air mail
Par avion

When the object is covered, paint a final layer of watered-down white glue over the surface to give a shiny finish.

Instead of using paper and cardboard for making a collage, try using fabric scraps and pieces of yarn and ribbon. Use special fabric glue to glue the pieces of fabric. Experiment with pleating, crumpling and weaving.

Look for fabrics with interesting textures such as velvet, felt, canvas and fake fur. Try mixing different types of fabric and think about colors and patterns.

Here is an idea for making a fabric collage using lots of different techniques. We added buttons and beads but you may have other ideas.

You can use fabric glue, pins or staples to attach the pieces of fabric to the backing.

Look in craft stores, lumber yards, and do-it-yourself frame shops for scraps of wood. You may find old picture frames, wooden handles, and old carvings. Use a piece of fairly soft wood for the base.

Ask a grown-up to saw the pieces of wood to the lengths you need and to help you glue or nail them down.

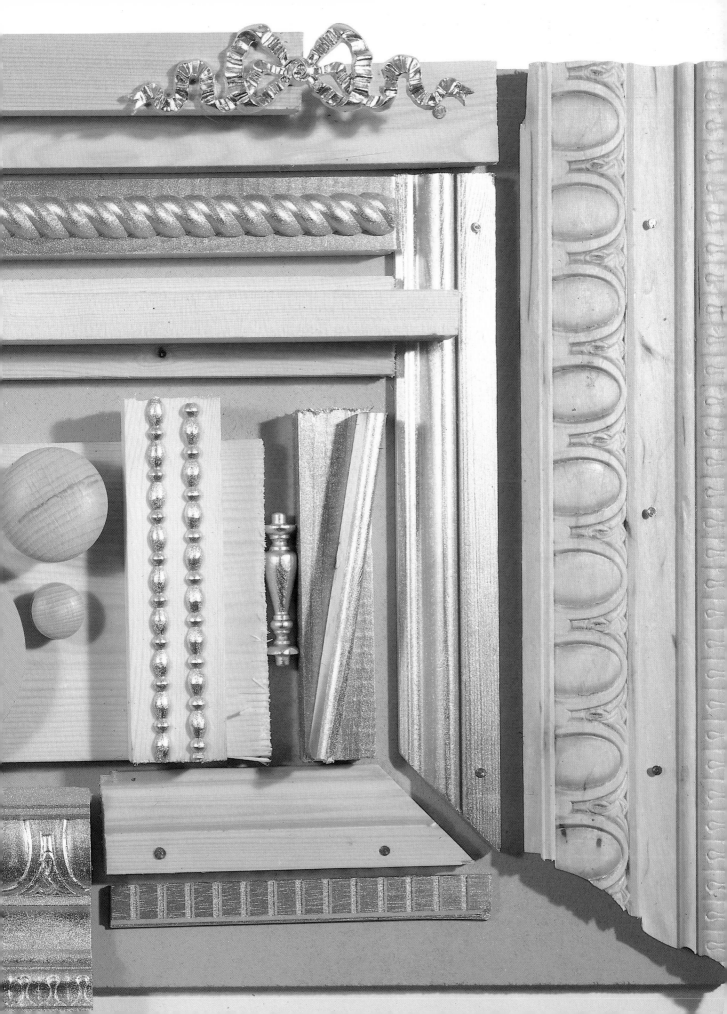

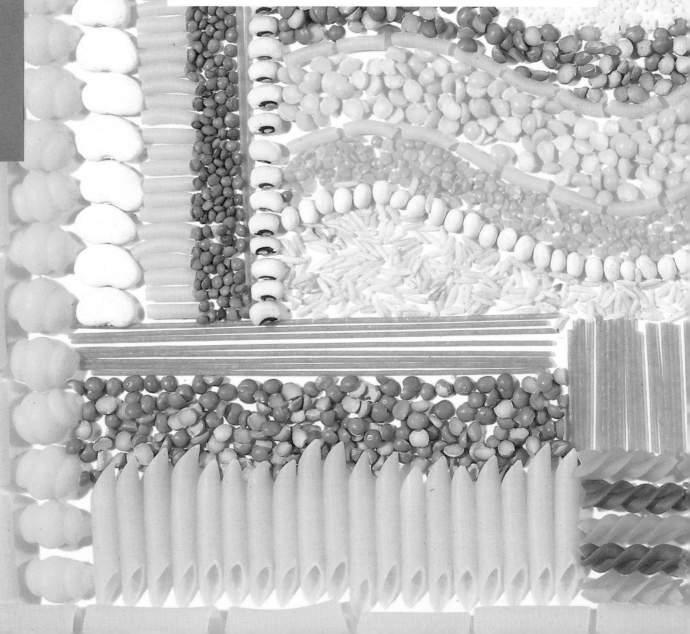

This collage was made from a mixture of dry pasta, beans, peas and rice. Look for interesting shapes and colors.

Use a piece of strong cardboard for the backing. You will need to use quite a lot of glue. Cover a small area at a time with glue and attach the dry food.

It is a good idea to sketch your idea out first on a piece of paper to use as a guide.

Here are some ideas for making collages that are delicious to eat. Use bread or crackers for bases. Try cutting the bread into shapes with a pastry cutter.

Look for brightly colored food for toppings such as tomatoes, cheese, peppers and fruit. Ask a grown-up to help slice the food. Arrange it carefully on your bread or cracker bases.

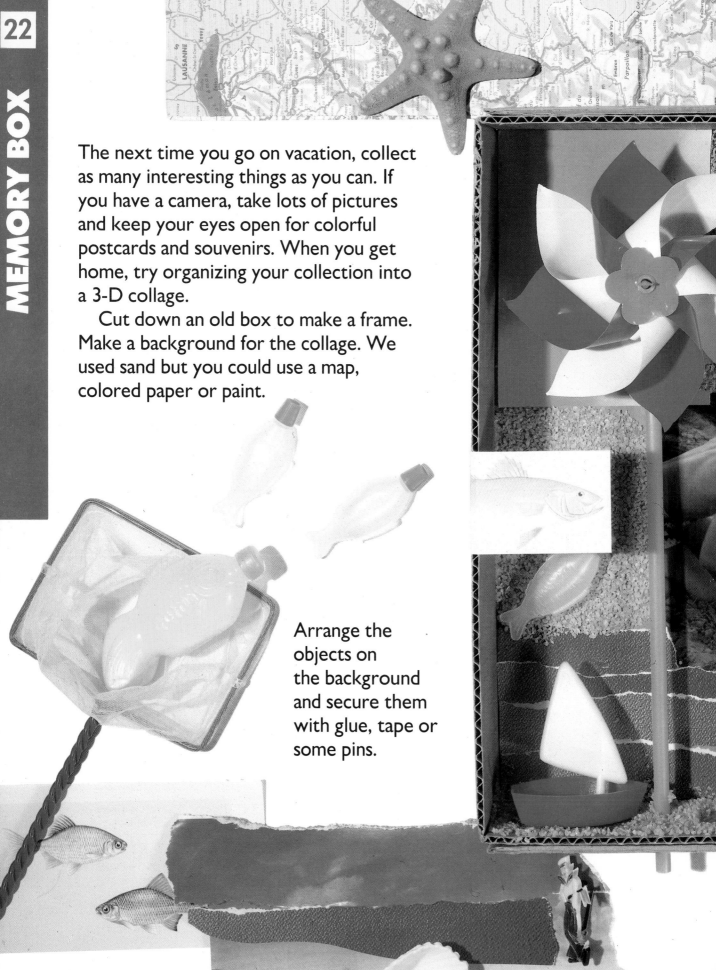

The next time you go on vacation, collect as many interesting things as you can. If you have a camera, take lots of pictures and keep your eyes open for colorful postcards and souvenirs. When you get home, try organizing your collection into a 3-D collage.

Cut down an old box to make a frame. Make a background for the collage. We used sand but you could use a map, colored paper or paint.

Arrange the objects on the background and secure them with glue, tape or some pins.

A giant collage is ideal for a party or as decoration for your room. For the backing use craft paper, which you can buy in craft stores. Sketch out your design first.

aint the background and glue
n paper and fabric using some
f the techniques shown on
e next pages.

Once you have decided on a theme for your giant collage, look for lots of different textured papers and fabrics. Think carefully about colors and patterns. You may get some ideas from the things we have used in our book.

To make paper stand out from the background, make tabs by folding the edges under.

To make neat folds in paper, use a ruler and scoring tool to mark the folds first.

This is an idea for a collage that you do not need to glue down. In fact, you can move things around to change the look of the collage and you can add to it when your collection grows.

Find a cardboard or wooden box that your collection will fit into. If the box is too deep, ask a grown-up to cut down the sides. Slot strips of cardboard or wood into the box to make sections.

Group your collection into different shapes and colors. This will work for any collection – buttons, beads, toys, dried flowers.

This collage is based on a food theme. Make a collection of food labels, pictures from magazines and newspapers, and empty seed packages. (If you take a label off an unopened can, put a new label on.) Use the side of a printed corrugated box for the backing. You can cut round food shapes or cut squares or rectangles from the pictures.

Try raising some of the shapes from the backing by first gluing them onto thick cardboard.